Far North
in the **Arctic**

Far North in the Arctic

COUNTING ALASKA'S ANIMALS

Cory Cooper Hansen

Illustrated by
Kathryn Kunz Finney

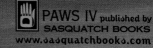

PAWS IV published by
SASQUATCH BOOKS
www.sasquatchbooks.com

Far north in the Arctic 'neath the midnight sun

Lived an old mother beluga and her little calf **1**.

"Sing," said the mother. "I sing," said the **one**.

So they sang and they swam 'neath the midnight sun.

Far north in the Arctic  where you'll find an igloo

Lived a mother polar bear and her little cubs **2**.

"Growl," said the mother. "We growl," said the **two**.

So they growled and they prowled where you'll find an igloo.

Far north in the Arctic by a cold, cold sea

Lived a mother snowshoe hare and her leverets **3**.

"Jump," said the mother. "We jump," said the **three**.

So they jumped and they thumped by a cold, cold sea.

Far north in the Arctic near an icy shore

Lived a wrinkled mother walrus and her nieces **4**.

"Bellow," said the mother. "We bellow," said the **four**.

So they bellowed and they barked near an icy shore.

Far north in the Arctic where the air is alive

Lived a mother arctic wolf and her little pups **5**.

"Yip," said the mother. "We yip," said the **five**.

So they yipped and they yapped where the air is alive.

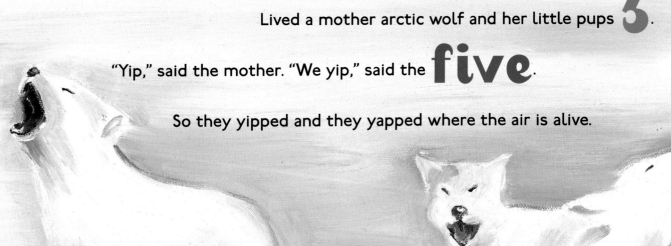

Far north in the Arctic by the light of oil wicks

Lived a mother snowy owl and her owlets **6**.

"Swoop," said the mother. "We swoop," said the **six**.

So they swooped and they shadowed by the light of oil wicks.

Far north in the Arctic in a red and green heaven

Lived a ptarmigan mom and her little chicks 7.

"Fly," said the mother. "We fly," said the seven.

So they flew and they grew in a red and green heaven.

Far north in the Arctic by the Bering Strait

Lived a mother arctic fox and her little kits 8.

"Pounce," said the mother. "We pounce," said the **eight**.

So they pounced and they bounced by the Bering Strait.

Far north in the Arctic in an undersnow line

Lived a plump mother lemming and her little lemmies .

"Dig," said the mother. "We dig," said the **nine**.

So they dug and they hugged in an undersnow line.

Far north in the Arctic where the dogs help the men

Lived a young mother husky and her little pups **10**.

"Pull," said the mother. "We pull," said the **ten**.

So they geed and they hawed where the dogs help the men.

"The Land of the Midnight Sun" is a name given to the Arctic because the sun shines day and night during the summer. **Beluga whales** migrate to the far north during this time to give birth. The babies are born gray so that they blend with the color of the ocean. They don't turn completely white until they are about six years old. Belugas love to dive and splash, but their favorite thing to do is sing. Sailors call these whales "sea canaries" because their songs can be heard even above the water.

The first people of the Arctic—the Inuit—learned to build snow houses, called igloos, from **polar bears**. The great white bears would dig caves in snowdrifts for shelter, and the Inuit found they could stay warm and dry inside snow too. Igloos were built on long hunting journeys as the Inuit followed the herds of animals they needed to survive. Nowadays, most Inuit live in modern houses in settlements. Polar bears only come into town to look for food when they are hungry and seals are scarce!

Arctic hares live in large colonies. Like some other Arctic animals, hares turn white in the winter, but even then the tips of their ears stay black. Their ears are shorter than other hares so they lose less body heat. Another way they keep warm is by growing thick fur on the top and the bottom of their feet. If Arctic hares can't see as far as they want, they jump straight up into the air. Maybe they are looking for their favorite food: a piece of arctic willow.

Walrus are cousins of seals, but they are much bigger, and the males have two large tusks that are really front teeth. The tusks help separate shellfish from stones when the walrus is looking for food on the ocean floor. The females like to cuddle close together in large herds on ice packs that float in the Arctic Ocean. There they like to sunbathe, look after their babies, and talk to each other. Walrus can make all kinds of noises besides bellows and barks. They roar, clang, click, and even whistle.

The air in the Arctic can be so cold that breath freezes into snow mist. **Arctic wolves** send messages to their families by howling in the icy air. Families are close and wolves will take care of another that is sick or injured. Mothers even leave their pups with a babysitter wolf. The pups spend a lot of time running, chasing, digging, and playing so that they will grow up to be strong hunters. When they get tired of all that, they play a favorite game: jump on the babysitter.

Both people and animals have had to adapt to the harsh Arctic climate. The early Inuit needed warmth and light, so they used oil wick lamps in their igloos. The lamps were carved from soft stone, blubber was cooked down to oil, and a wick was made from dried moss. **Snowy owls** use moss too. If there is enough, they will use it for a nest. If not, they lay their eggs right on the ground! With their big eyes, they can hunt day or night. If a lemming sees the shadow of an owl, he needs to run fast because snowy owls like to hunt lemmings.

The northern lights (aurora borealis) dance across the Arctic skies with red, green, white, and even yellow streaks of color. These ribbons of light provide a beautiful background for the state bird of Alaska: the **ptarmigan**. Ptarmigan spend most of the time on the ground, but they can fly perfectly well. This bird is one of the few that lives its whole life in the cold of the Arctic. Eggs are laid in a bare hollow on the ground. The babies grow up to eat leaves, shoots and, in the fall, berries.

The Bering Strait is the passage of icy seawater that separates Alaska from Russia. **Arctic foxes** live on both sides of the water. They are grayish-brown in the summer and white as snow in the winter. Blending into the snow lets them sneak up and pounce on their prey: lemmings, insects, and birds. They like lemmings the best but, if they are hungry enough, they will even eat seaweed! Like other Arctic animals that have southern cousins, these foxes have shorter ears and snouts to help them save body heat.

Lemmings are plump little mouse-like creatures that dig tunnels through the snow and into the soil. Their hard-packed snow tunnels don't melt as fast as the rest of the snow in the spring, so undersnow "lines" are left on the ground. Lemming homes have rest areas and nesting rooms where they snuggle to keep warm. The best part about their underground homes is that the food grows right down to them! Lemmings eat the thick mat of roots and stems that grow into the soil.

Dogsled drivers are called mushers. They shout "gee" when they need the dogs to turn right and "haw" when they want them to turn left. A **husky** is one kind of sled dog. The native Inuit used dogs to pull hunting sleds across the ice in search of seals. Most people who live in the Arctic today use snowmobiles, but dogsleds are still used for fun and races. The dogs can live outside all year long because they have two layers of fur to keep them warm. They burrow into the snow, curl up tight, and dream about running.

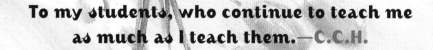

**To my students, who continue to teach me
as much as I teach them.—C.C.H.**

**For Arthur and Madison,
my inspiration for my paintings.—K.K.F.**

Printed in China
Published by Sasquatch Books
Distributed by Publishers Group West

11 10 09 08 07 06 05 04   6 5 4 3 2 1

Book design: Kate Basart
Production: Bill Quinby

Library of Congress Cataloging-in-Publication Data is available

ISBN: 1-57061-371-0
Sasquatch Books • 119 South Main Street, Suite 400 • Seattle, WA 98104 • 206/467-4300
www.sasquatchbooks.com • custserv@sasquatchbooks.com